Little Mix

Test Your
Super-Fan Status

T0116793

Written by Jack Thorpe

Edited by Imogen Williams
Designed by Janine Spencer
Cover design by Angie Allison

Picture Acknowledgements:
Front cover: Jon Kopaloff/Getty Images

Picture section:
Page 1: Ben Gabbe/Getty Images
Page 2: Dave J Hogan/Getty Images
Page 3: Kevin Mazur/Getty Images
Page 4: Kevin Mazur/Getty Images
Page 5: Dave J Hogan/Getty Images
Page 6-7: Kevin Mazur/Getty Images
Page 8: Eamonn McCormack/Getty Images

Published in Great Britain in 2018 by Buster Books,
an imprint of Michael O'Mara Books Limited,
9 Lion Yard, Tremadoc Road, London SW4 7NQ

W www.mombooks.com/buster   f Buster Books   🐦 @BusterBooks

Text copyright © Buster Books 2018
Artwork adapted from www.shutterstock.com

A CIP catalogue record for this book is available from the British Library.

ISBN: 978–1–78055–604–8

**PLEASE NOTE: This book is not affiliated with or endorsed
by Little Mix or any of their publishers or licencees.**

1 3 5 7 9 10 8 6 4 2

Printed and bound in November 2018 by CPI Group (UK) Ltd,
108 Beddington Lane, Croydon, CR0 4YY, United Kingdom.

Papers used by Buster Books are natural, recyclable products made
from wood grown in sustainable forests. The manufacturing processes
conform to the environmental regulations of the country of origin.

Little Mix

Test Your
Super-Fan Status

Buster Books

CONTENTS

ABOUT THIS BOOK

You're reading this because you are a huge Little Mix fan. You love everything about Jesy, Jade, Leigh-Anne and Perrie – from their catchy songs and epic dancing to their slick videos and super-sassy style. Quite simply, the girls are the greatest pop stars on the planet!

You probably remember the foursome getting together on *The X Factor*, their debut number one single and which video reached 300 million views first. Whether your fave tune is 'Black Magic', 'Power', 'Touch' or 'Wings', you'll spend hours singing their songs and copying all their dance moves. That's what it takes to become a true fan and a devoted Mixer.

But exactly how much do you know about Little Mix? This book is full of cool trivia, quizzes, puzzles and activities to test your super-fan status. Plus, there are eight awesome glossy photos showing off the singing superstars.

So put your favourite tunes on, grab a pen and find out how much you *really* know about Little Mix. You can check your answers on pages 91 to 96.

SUPER-FAN-TASTIC!

TO KICK OFF YOUR QUEST TO BE A LITTLE MIX
SUPER-FAN, HERE'S A QUICK QUIZ ALL ABOUT THE GIRLS.
JUST TICK A, B OR C TO ANSWER EACH QUESTION.
CHECK THE ANSWERS ON **PAGE 91**.

1. Who is the youngest member of Little Mix?
   a. Perrie
   b. Jesy
   c. Jade

2. Who is the oldest?
   a. Leigh-Anne
   b. Jade
   c. Jesy

3. On which date did the band release their first chart song as a download?
   a. 11th December, 2011
   b. 31st December, 2012
   c. 1st January, 2013

4. Which of these high street clothes stores has Little Mix launched a fashion range with?

   a. Superdry

   b. Primark

   c. H&M

5. What middle name do two of the girls both have?

   a. Emma

   b. Louise

   c. Elaine

6. Which pair are both originally from the north-east of England?

   a. Perrie & Jesy

   b. Leigh-Anne & Jesy

   c. Perrie & Jade

7. In which year did the group perform their first headline tour?

   a. 2011

   b. 2013

   c. 2015

8. Who was engaged to former One Direction star, Zayn Malik?

   a. Perrie

   b. Jade

   c. Leigh-Anne

9. Which music label are Little Mix signed to?
   a. Syco
   b. Universal
   c. Warner

10. When they first formed, which member was known for wearing cute ribbons in her hair?
    a. Jade
    b. Jesy
    c. Perrie

11. By the summer of 2018, how many albums had Little Mix released?
    a. 2
    b. 4
    c. 6

12. Which of these artists has Little Mix supported on tour?
    a. Drake
    b. Dua Lipa
    c. Ariana Grande

FACT OR FIB:
JESY

ONLY SIX OF THESE NINE STATEMENTS ABOUT
JESY ARE TRUE. PUT A TICK IN THE BOX BESIDE EACH
STATEMENT THAT YOU THINK IS FACT AND A CROSS
IF IT'S A FIB. CHECK YOUR ANSWERS ON **PAGE 91**.

1. Her full first name is actually Jessica.

2. She speaks fluent Spanish.

3. Jesy says her nickname is Jesminda.

4. Her favourite colours are black and red.

5. George Ezra is her cousin.

6. She has a skull tattoo on her arm.

7. She went to theatre school with Rita Ora.

8. Jesy once worked in a bakery.

9. Jesy loves eating Indian food.

THE LITTLE MIX STORY

FIND OUT HOW THE POP PRINCESSES BECAME ONE OF THE WORLD'S BIGGEST GROUPS. READ THEIR AMAZING STORY AND TRY TO FILL IN THE MISSING WORDS. THE ANSWERS CAN BE FOUND ON **PAGE 91**.

It was on a hit British TV show, called .... , where the girls would first meet in 2011. Jesy Nelson, Jade Thirlwall, Leigh-Anne Pinnock and Perrie Edwards appeared as solo singers in the wannabe pop star auditions and tried really hard to impress the judges.

They made it through to the boot camp stage of the TV programme. Then, the judges had the brilliant idea to put the four together in a group. .... were born! But that actually wasn't their original name – for the first few weeks they were known as ....

Over the next three months, Little Mix got better and better. They performed amazing songs and reached the final, where the TV audience voted them the winners.

Their first chart release was ....

and it zoomed straight to number .... in the UK chart.

The next year was massive for the pop foursome. Their second song, 'Wings', got to number one. Little Mix fans finally got their hands on the group's first album, called

....

Nearly two years after the band formed, they released their second album. It was called *Salute* and featured awesome tunes like 'Move' and 'Little Me'. In 2015 they had their

biggest hit single so far, with the song 'Black .... '. It enjoyed three weeks at the top of the charts!

The band's fourth album, *Glory* .... , finally gave them their first number one album. They picked up

lots of pop prizes too, winning a .... for their epic tune 'Shout Out To My Ex'. Little Mix look like they'll be creating mega music and putting on top tours for years to come.

TWEET HEARTS

THE LITTLE MIX MEMBERS HAVE THOUSANDS OF TWITTER FOLLOWERS. READ THE TWEETS BELOW AND GUESS WHICH BAND MEMBER POSTED THEM. GO TO **PAGE 91** FOR THE ANSWER.

dancing like nobody was watching

Meet me where the sky touches the sea

Being locked in a studio vocal booth for over 10hrs really does bring out a crazy side

my two fave things... making music and eating chips

Hiya my little pudding pies... I love you! Just know I'm sending you ALL virtual squishy hugs & kisses for being the most amazing humans ever.

The mystery Tweeter is ....

ART ATTACK

LITTLE MIX HAVE AMAZING ARTWORK AND DESIGNS FOR
THEIR ALBUM COVERS AND WEBSITE. CAN YOU DESIGN A COOL
NEW ALBUM COVER FOR THE BAND IN THE BOX BELOW?

SONG SCRAMBLE

TO BE A TRUE SUPER-FAN, YOU'VE GOT TO KNOW
ALL OF LITTLE MIX'S BIGGEST HITS. CAN YOU
UNSCRAMBLE THESE MIXED-UP SONG NAMES?
GO TO **PAGE 91** TO PEEK AT THE ANSWERS.

1. 'GINWS'

....

2. 'ERPOW'

....

3. 'COHUT'

....

4. 'THUSO UTO OT YM XE'

....

5. 'BKCAL GAMIC'

....

6. 'HIRA'

....

7. 'LATEUS'

....

8. 'VOEL EM KEIL OYU'

....

9. 'RECSET EVLO NOGS'

....

Which is your favourite song?

....

TOTALLY
MIXED UP!

WHO SAID IT?

CAN YOU GUESS WHO SAID EACH OF THESE QUOTES?
GO TO **PAGE 92** TO SEE IF YOU'RE CORRECT.

1. 'We don't get nervous, unless it's like, The Brit Awards, or *The X Factor* or a big live television show.'

Who said it? ....

2. 'I get called Jade a lot.'

Who said it? ....

3. 'We were meant to go to the zoo today but we didn't have enough time.'

Who said it? ....

4. 'I'm going to go to Cheesecake Factory and order three cheesecakes!'

Who said it? ....

5. 'I used to love Justin Bieber, but not so much anymore.'

Who said it? ....

6. 'I've had boyfriends that my friends hated.'

Who said it? ....

7. 'It's never nice to break a heart.'

Who said it? ....

8. 'We love to wear what we want to wear. We want everyone else to feel like they can be confident whatever they are wearing as well.'

Who said it? ....

9. 'When we were young girls we dreamed of being a singer.'

Who said it? ....

10. 'Who would've thought you could make a Brussels sprout taste insane?'

Who said it? ....

CAR-RAZY CHOICES

YOU'RE ON A CAR JOURNEY AND CAN ONLY LISTEN TO ONE OF THESE LITTLE MIX TRACK LISTS, BUT WHICH WILL YOU CHOOSE? TICK YOUR CHOICE OF 1, 2, 3 OR 4.

TRACK LIST 1 ☐

Cannonball
Little Me
Move
How Ya Doin'
Salute

TRACK LIST 3 ☐

Hair
Love Me Like You
Secret Love Song
Grown
Touch

TRACK LIST 2 ☐

Wings
Power
Shout Out To My Ex
Black Magic
Word Up

TRACK LIST 4 ☐

Only You
No More Sad Songs
Oops
Reggaetón Lento
DNA

YOUR ULTIMATE BFF

WANT TO DISCOVER WHICH LITTLE MIX HERO COULD BE YOUR BFF? TAKE THIS QUIZ TO FIND OUT. THE POP STAR PAL YOU'RE MOST LIKE IS REVEALED ON **PAGE 22.**

1. What's your fave stage style and look?
   a. Bold and a bit rock chick
   b. Fresh, bright and fun
   c. Funky and urban
   d. Sassy and sophisticated

2. Which words best describe you and your personality?
   a. Strong, outgoing, passionate
   b. Quiet, cute, friendly
   c. Determined, stylish, team player
   d. Confident, goofy, trustworthy

3. If you could choose one of these meals for dinner tonight, what would it be?
   a. Curry
   b. Lasagne
   c. Fajitas
   d. Spaghetti and meatballs

4. If you were an animal or creature, what would you be?
   a. A tiger
   b. A mermaid
   c. A fox
   d. A meerkat

5. What do you take with you to read on holiday?
   a. An autobiography of a pop queen, like Beyoncé
   b. A book about football, because it's your fave sport
   c. A fashion magazine
   d. A travel guide

6. You have time to relax and listen to an album. What do you choose?
   a. Beyoncé's album, 4
   b. *Back to Black* by Amy Winehouse
   c. *Something* by Mariah Carey
   d. Britney Spears' greatest hits

7. What's your ideal way to spend your birthday?
   a. Going to a gig and staying up late
   b. Taking your three besties out for dinner
   c. A karaoke party with friends
   d. Going home to see your family

8. It's a home movie night, but what do you put on?

   a. *The Notebook*

   b. A classic Disney film – they're the best

   c. *Love Actually*

   d. A funny rom-com movie

9. If you could buy your best friend anything for Christmas, what would it be?

   a. Stage theatre lessons

   b. Something extravagant, like a car

   c. A cute pet dog

   d. A holiday for both of you

10. What's your favourite accessory?

   a. Dark-coloured nails and eye-catching rings

   b. Gorgeous shoes – you have so many pairs

   c. A designer handbag – you're a designer kind of girl

   d. A hat – anything from baseball caps to cowboy hats

11. What type of games do you like to play?

   a. A spooky, mystery, Halloween-based game

   b. Football

   c. Dress-up games, as you love new outfits

   d. A fun game, like Hide and Seek

TURN OVER TO FIND OUT!

THE RESULTS

COUNT UP YOUR SCORES TO REVEAL YOUR BFF.

MOSTLY As ... YOUR BFF IS JESY

You're a bit spicy, feisty and a proper rock and pop queen. Even your favourite Indian food is fiery, like you! You love to express yourself, whether on stage or talking to friends, and you can be 100% relied on to help others.

MOSTLY Bs ... YOUR BFF IS JADE

Sometimes it's tricky for your friends to figure you out – you love Disney princesses as well as football. You're a cracking laugh to be around and treating those close to you is very important. Jade and you would be best buds!

MOSTLY Cs ... YOUR BFF IS LEIGH-ANNE

Just like Leigh-Anne, fashion and performing rule your world. You make time for cute things too, like pet dogs and fun films, and if any of your pals have a problem you're always there to help them out. Nice one.

MOSTLY Ds ... YOUR BFF IS PERRIE

You and Perrie would get on so well. You both have a silly and jokey side. You'd enjoy going on holidays together and watching funny films. Travelling the world would be fun – perhaps a trip to Italy for traditional pasta and pizza!

TWEET HEARTS

THE GIRLS LOVE TO TWEET. GUESS WHICH SINGER SENT THESE TWEETS AND WRITE HER NAME AT THE BOTTOM OF THE PAGE. FIND OUT THE ANSWER ON **PAGE 92**.

we see all your messages daily and we can't wait to share this music with you. It will be worth the wait!

....

love a good studio sesh ♥

....

Patience is a virtue! Lol

....

Be unapologetic when it comes to standing up for something you believe in..

....

Summer Tour Lovin... ♥

....

The mystery Tweeter is ....

CODE CRACKER

IF YOU WANT ACCESS TO A TOP SECRET LITTLE MIX GIG, YOU MUST USE YOUR DETECTIVE SKILLS TO CRACK THE CLUES BELOW. THE ANSWERS ARE REVEALED ON **PAGE 92**.

The secret gig is in a big city not far from where Jesy grew up.

Which city is it? ....

Little Mix have collaborated with a superstar. Cross out all the Bs, Ds, Hs and Gs to find the mystery performer.

N	B	G	I	C	G	H	K	D
G	I	H	D	B	M	I	H	G
H	N	G	B	A	J	D	D	H

Who is the mystery performer? ....

....

You're inside the venue, but you need a special combination to open the door. Put together all the answers to these three questions to get the seven-digit code.

1. How old did Jesy and Leigh-Anne both become on their birthdays in 2018?
   a. 25
   b. 27
   c. 30

2. The UK chart position that their first song, 'Cannonball', reached.
   a. 9
   b. 5
   c. 1

3. In which year was the *Glory Days* album released?
   a. 2016
   b. 2014
   c. 2012

What's the combination? ....

FACT OR FIB: LEIGH-ANNE

ONLY FIVE OF THESE NINE STATEMENTS ABOUT LEIGH-ANNE ARE TRUE. PUT A TICK IN THE BOX BESIDE EACH STATEMENT THAT YOU THINK IS FACT AND A CROSS IF IT'S A FIB. CHECK YOUR ANSWERS ON **PAGE 92**.

1. Leigh-Anne loves to post pictures and blog about fashion.

2. She grew up in High Wycombe, Buckinghamshire, in England.

3. The singer used to be in a group called Girls Aloud.

4. Her nicknames are Leigh-Leigh and Fresh Princess.

5. Leigh-Anne used to work as a Pizza Hut waitress.

6. When she was 15 she appeared on *Britain's Got Talent*.

7. She began dating footballer Andre Gray in 2016.

8. Leigh-Anne's childhood dream was to swim at the Olympics.

9. One of her hobbies is collecting old paintings.

SUPER STAR SOLVER

READ THE CLUES AND SEE HOW LONG IT TAKES YOU TO FILL IN THIS CROSSWORD. THE ANSWERS CAN BE FOUND ON **PAGE 92**.

ACROSS

1. Little Mix song title, plus birds have these (5)

2. The name of Little Mix's first official book (5,2,3)

3. One of four singles released in 2017, 'No More Sad _ _ _ _ _' (5)

DOWN

4. The group's third album, *Get _ _ _ _ _* (5)

5. Their first number one album (5,4)

6. She was once engaged to Jake Roshe (4)

WHO'S YOUR LITTLE MIX STYLE TWIN?

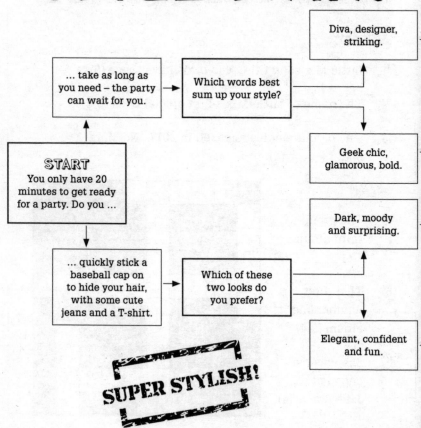

Diva, designer, striking.

... take as long as you need – the party can wait for you.

Which words best sum up your style?

Geek chic, glamorous, bold.

START
You only have 20 minutes to get ready for a party. Do you ...

Dark, moody and surprising.

... quickly stick a baseball cap on to hide your hair, with some cute jeans and a T-shirt.

Which of these two looks do you prefer?

Elegant, confident and fun.

SUPER STYLISH!

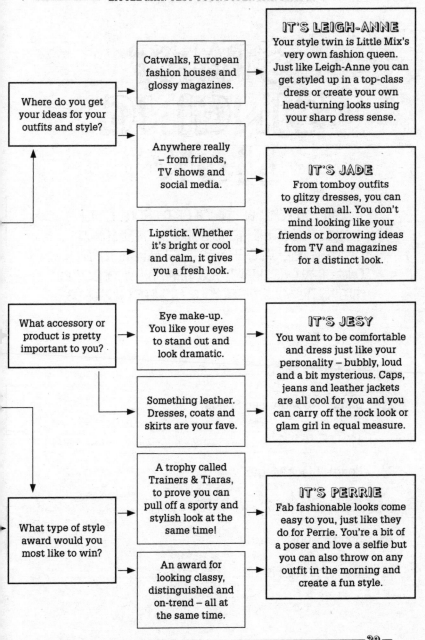

Where do you get your ideas for your outfits and style?

Catwalks, European fashion houses and glossy magazines.

IT'S LEIGH-ANNE
Your style twin is Little Mix's very own fashion queen. Just like Leigh-Anne you can get styled up in a top-class dress or create your own head-turning looks using your sharp dress sense.

Anywhere really – from friends, TV shows and social media.

IT'S JADE
From tomboy outfits to glitzy dresses, you can wear them all. You don't mind looking like your friends or borrowing ideas from TV and magazines for a distinct look.

Lipstick. Whether it's bright or cool and calm, it gives you a fresh look.

What accessory or product is pretty important to you?

Eye make-up. You like your eyes to stand out and look dramatic.

IT'S JESY
You want to be comfortable and dress just like your personality – bubbly, loud and a bit mysterious. Caps, jeans and leather jackets are all cool for you and you can carry off the rock look or glam girl in equal measure.

Something leather. Dresses, coats and skirts are your fave.

What type of style award would you most like to win?

A trophy called Trainers & Tiaras, to prove you can pull off a sporty and stylish look at the same time!

IT'S PERRIE
Fab fashionable looks come easy to you, just like they do for Perrie. You're a bit of a poser and love a selfie but you can also throw on any outfit in the morning and create a fun style.

An award for looking classy, distinguished and on-trend – all at the same time.

START SINGING NOW

CAN YOU REMEMBER WHICH OF THE FOUR LITTLE MIX STARS IS THE FIRST TO SING IN THESE SONGS? WRITE PERRIE, JADE, JESY OR LEIGH-ANNE AFTER EACH SONG, OR 'ALL OF THEM' IF YOU THINK THE WHOLE GROUP BEGINS THE SONG. CHECK YOUR ANSWERS ON **PAGE 93**.

1. Song: 'Touch'

   The first to sing is: ....

2. Song: 'No More Sad Songs'

   The first to sing is: ....

3. Song: 'Black Magic'

   The first to sing is: ....

4. Song: 'Oops'

   The first to sing is: ....

5. Song: 'Love Me Like You'

The first to sing is: ....

6. Song: 'Hair'

The first to sing is: ....

7. Song: 'Wings'

The first to sing is: ....

8. Song: 'Cannonball'

The first to sing is: ....

9. Song: 'DNA'

The first to sing is: ....

10. Song: 'Secret Love Song'

The first to sing is: ....

WOULD YOU RATHER ...

IMAGINE HAVING THE CHANCE TO DANCE WITH LITTLE MIX, SING ALONGSIDE THEM OR JUST HANG OUT AND BE FRIENDS. WELL, NOW YOU CAN! PICK WHICH OF THE THINGS BELOW YOU'D RATHER DO. WHY NOT SEE WHAT YOUR FRIENDS CHOOSE TOO AND COMPARE YOUR ANSWERS.

Would you rather ...

Have front row tickets to their biggest concert? 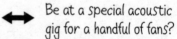 Be at a special acoustic gig for a handful of fans?

Go clothes shopping with the band for a day? 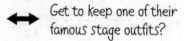 Get to keep one of their famous stage outfits?

Party with the girls at the Brit Awards afterparty? 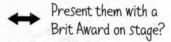 Present them with a Brit Award on stage?

Appear in a magazine photoshoot with Little Mix? 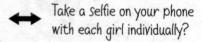 Take a selfie on your phone with each girl individually?

Go for dinner at a top restaurant with them? 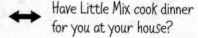 Have Little Mix cook dinner for you at your house?

Take them to school with you for the day? Spend the school holidays chilling with them?

Go to Perrie's birthday party? Invite Perrie to your birthday party?

Spend all day texting and messaging the group? Have a ten-minute Skype with just one of the girls?

Appear in the latest Little Mix video? Sing on the latest Little Mix song?

Have a Little Mix perfume named after you? Have a Little Mix song named after you?

Ask Jade for make-up tips? Ask Jesy for hairstyle tips?

Get a singing lesson from Perrie? Get a dancing lesson from Leigh-Anne?

Play Truth or Dare with the girls? Play computer games with the girls?

Reveal your cringiest moment to them? Make them tell you their own crazy cringes?

TWEET HEARTS

DID JESY, JADE, LEIGH-ANNE OR PERRIE POST THESE
TWEETS ON SOCIAL MEDIA? HAVE A LOOK THROUGH THEM
AND TAKE A GUESS, THEN CHECK YOUR ANSWER ON **PAGE 93**.

🐦 a great mind must be androgynous.

....

🐦 WOMEN ARE MORE THAN MUSES. Shout out to all the
amazing women past and present who fight for the rights
and freedom of women

....

🐦 Song writing again today. What concepts would you like
to hear us sing about? :)

....

🐦 ONLY YOU. out now. I can only record my best if there's
a cuppa in the booth with me

....

🐦 BEYONCÉ. AT. COACHELLA. WAS. THE. BEST. THING.
I. HAVE. EVER. WITNESSED. I just watched history in the
making. #BeyChella

....

The mystery Tweeter is ....

STARRING ROLE

YOUR STAR SIGN SAYS A LOT ABOUT WHAT
TYPE OF PERSON YOU ARE. IT ALSO GIVES YOU AN IDEA
OF THE JOB YOU COULD DO IN 'TEAM LITTLE MIX'.

ARIES (21ST MARCH - 20TH APRIL)

If you're born under the sign Aries, you're an independent
person with a strong will to succeed. Not everyone likes
your competitive nature, but even though you're determined
you are also a caring team player.

Your Little Mix job: Tour manager

When Little Mix tour the world, they rely on you to make
sure they arrive where they need to be and everything is
in top working order. If Jade, Jesy, Perrie or Leigh-Anne
have an issue, you'll sort it out.

TAURUS (21ST APRIL - 21ST MAY)

If you're a Taurus then you like to look after your appearance
and give off good vibes. You're a calm person who enjoys
chatting and relaxing backstage. Having a good time with
friends is important to you.

Your Little Mix job: Make-up artist

You always look beautiful and do a great job of making Little
Mix appear stunning on TV and stage. When the girls are in
the make-up chair they always have a giggle with you.

GEMINI (22ND MAY - 21ST JUNE)

A Gemini is someone who wants to know lots of things – you love collecting information and news. You're clever and can quickly communicate to your friends what needs to be done and by when. You are also highly organized.

Your Little Mix job: Social media manager
You're never far from your phone or laptop and can update Instagram and websites in a flash! The group trusts you to get the best information out there for the fans to like and comment on.

CANCER (22ND JUNE - 23RD JULY)

Your star sign makes you a very caring person – you treat your friends just like family. Cancereans can be protective and, with a sharp memory as well, you enjoy reminding people of their jobs and roles.

Your Little Mix job: Head of security
From the moment they wake up to the second they fall asleep, your job is to keep Little Mix safe and together. From aeroplanes to studios and hotel rooms, no one gets close without your permission.

LEO (24TH JULY - 23RD AUGUST)

Being a Leo means you enjoy leading your friends and inspiring them to reach their goals. Your strong personality makes you popular. When you have some spare money, your first thought is to treat your friends and family.

Your Little Mix job: Band manager

Little Mix wouldn't want anyone else to manage their daily diary. You are strict when you need to be, but if the group are tired or stressed a few words of wisdom gets them back on track.

VIRGO (24TH AUGUST - 23RD SEPTEMBER)

As a Virgo you don't like being the centre of attention. You're much happier sorting out other people's problems and putting your clever thinking into practise. You never waste anything and get the best deals and value for money.

Your Little Mix job: Financial assistant

That means you look after all the cash. Little Mix never have money worries because you do a great job with their earnings. You make sure credit cards are used wisely.

LIBRA (24TH SEPTEMBER - 23RD OCTOBER)

Persuading others and talking sense are your strengths. You'll never just sit on the fence or let others sway you. Libras are often sensitive, caring and diplomatic when sorting out problems.

Your Little Mix job: Public relations officer

When Little Mix face the media or appear in public, you make them look and feel amazing. You help other writers create great stories about the girls for magazines and websites. A good image in the fans' eyes is vital to you.

SCORPIO (24TH OCTOBER - 22ND NOVEMBER)

'Loyal' is the word used to describe a Scorpio. You can be trusted with a secret and your hard-working attitude is valued by your close friends. If you think someone has done a bad thing, you'll look for the facts before making a big decision.

Your Little Mix job: Personal assistant

Little Mix will come to you if they have any worries, because they know you'll soon sort them out. You speak to each of them every day and do all sorts of jobs, from charging their phones to booking restaurants.

SAGITTARIUS (23RD NOVEMBER - 21ST DECEMBER)

You like to live life on the edge and don't mind taking the odd risk, although you'd never put anyone in danger. As a Sagittarius you're full of enthusiasm and challenge others to work hard.

Your Little Mix job: Choreographer

Teaching Little Mix some slick dance moves is what you're about. Jesy and the gang love it when you come up with new ideas, routines and crazy numbers with their backing dancers.

CAPRICORN (22ND DECEMBER - 20TH JANUARY)

You are driven by deadlines and are extremely professional in life. This doesn't make you boring, but patience and time management are your major strengths. You trust a small group of people with important jobs.

Your Little Mix job: Contract negotiator
The stadiums Little Mix play at, the commercial deals they sign and any endorsements are your responsibility. If a deal isn't right for the group and their fans, you won't be signing it!

AQUARIUS (21ST JANUARY - 19TH FEBRUARY)
If something is wrong, you're not afraid to tell someone. You fix problems quickly and believe that people should share responsibility and make decisions together. You like new things, new gadgets and new ways of working.

Your Little Mix job: Producer

The quality of Little Mix's recordings and studio material is all down to you. You have a very important job and must make sure the group has best-selling hits and albums. You know how to get the best out of new recording technology.

PISCES (20TH FEBRUARY - 20TH MARCH)
You have a real artistic side and expressing yourself through music, dance or craft puts a smile on your face. You will always listen to other opinions and when your friends are happy, you're happy too.

Your Little Mix job: Artistic director
You have a big say in what the group should look like, what their stage designs are and any album artwork and photoshoots. The girls really value your 'arty' eye and attention to detail.

SUPER SINGING

YOU'RE A GOOD SINGER AND FANCY AUDITIONING TO BE THE FIFTH LITTLE MIX MEMBER. BUT WHAT'S YOUR SONG STYLE LIKE? CHOOSE YOUR ANSWERS AND SEE WHICH OF THE GIRLS YOU'RE MOST LIKE.

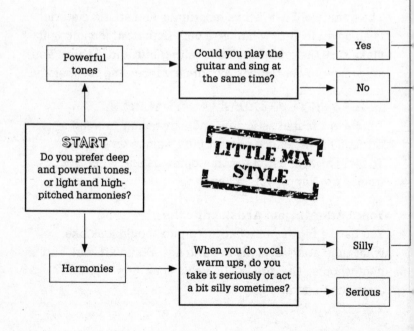

START
Do you prefer deep and powerful tones, or light and high-pitched harmonies?

Powerful tones

Could you play the guitar and sing at the same time?

Yes

No

LITTLE MIX STYLE

Harmonies

When you do vocal warm ups, do you take it seriously or act a bit silly sometimes?

Silly

Serious

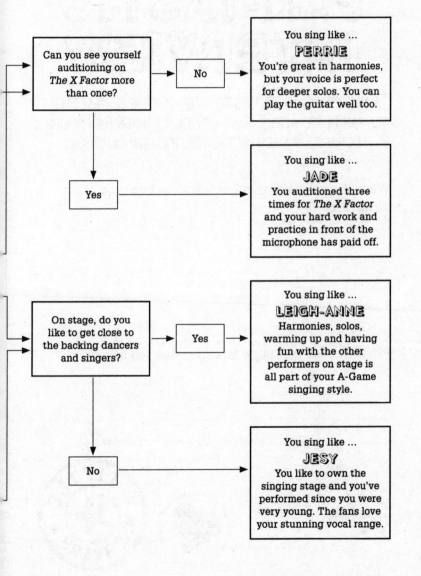

Can you see yourself auditioning on *The X Factor* more than once?

No

You sing like ...
PERRIE
You're great in harmonies, but your voice is perfect for deeper solos. You can play the guitar well too.

Yes

You sing like ...
JADE
You auditioned three times for *The X Factor* and your hard work and practice in front of the microphone has paid off.

On stage, do you like to get close to the backing dancers and singers?

Yes

You sing like ...
LEIGH-ANNE
Harmonies, solos, warming up and having fun with the other performers on stage is all part of your A-Game singing style.

No

You sing like ...
JESY
You like to own the singing stage and you've performed since you were very young. The fans love your stunning vocal range.

FAN-TASTIC INTERVIEW

A MUSIC MAGAZINE WANTS TO INTERVIEW THE BIGGEST LITTLE MIX FAN IN THE WORLD – AND OBVIOUSLY THAT'S YOU! SCRIBBLE DOWN YOUR AWESOME ANSWERS TO THEIR QUESTIONS.

When do you first remember seeing and hearing about Little Mix?

....

....

....

What was the first Little Mix song that you loved?

....

....

....

Who is your favourite member of the band, and why?

....

....

....

Who has the best style and look?

....

....

....

What is the best thing about a Little Mix concert?

....

....

....

How often do you watch them on YouTube?

....

....

....

What has been your top Little Mix moment so far?

....

....

....

Which other artists would you like them to perform with?

....

....

....

What are Little Mix fans like?

....

....

....

What do you hope Little Mix will be doing five years
from now?

....

....

....

ASK ANYTHING

THE SAME MUSIC MAGAZINE WANTS YOU TO INTERVIEW LITTLE MIX! ON THIS PAGE ARE SOME QUESTIONS YOU COULD USE. TURN OVER TO WRITE THE QUESTIONS YOU'D ASK - BE AS BOLD AND CREATIVE AS YOU LIKE.

♥ Who is the funniest girl in Little Mix?

♥ Would you like to star in a Hollywood movie all about your career?

♥ If you could tip a bucket of slime over any person, who would it be?

♥ What's your favourite pizza?

INTERVIEW TIP:
Asking each of the girls to reveal one funny fact the fans don't know about them could give some surprise answers

INTERVIEW TIP:
Listen carefully to Little Mix's answers and ask follow-up questions

WRITE DOWN THE QUESTIONS YOU'D ASK LEIGH-ANNE, PERRIE, JESY AND JADE.

1. ....
   ....

2. ....
   ....

3. ....
   ....

4. ....
   ....

5. ....
   ....

6. ....
   ....

7. ....
   ....

8. ....
   ....

TWEET HEARTS

THERE ARE POP STAR TWEETS AND MESSAGES FLYING ALL OVER THE PLACE. GUESS WHICH LITTLE MIX MEMBER WROTE THESE POSTS AND CHECK YOUR ANSWERS ON **PAGE 93**.

🐦 I ♥ PLATFORMS

....

🐦 I'll bring you flowers...

....

🐦 The support around #OnlyYou has been mental! Best fans ever

....

🐦 Something exciting is brewing

....

🐦 In my happy place! Can't wait for you lot to hear what we've got coming for ya!

....

The mystery Tweeter is ....

FACT OR FIB: PERRIE

ONLY SIX OF THESE NINE STATEMENTS ABOUT PERRIE
ARE TRUE. PUT A TICK IN THE BOX BESIDE EACH STATEMENT
THAT YOU THINK IS FACT AND A CROSS IF IT'S A FIB.
CHECK YOUR ANSWERS ON **PAGE 93**.

☐ 1. Both Perrie's parents were singers as well.

☐ 2. Her dad's nickname for her is 'Pep'.

☐ 3. Perrie's favourite colour is blue.

☐ 4. Perrie has a tattoo of a panda on her leg.

☐ 5. She once had a bite of a dog biscuit.

☐ 6. Perrie says she has fallen in love at first sight.

☐ 7. The singer has over 8 million Instagram followers.

☐ 8. Perrie is allergic to chocolate.

☐ 9. She used to keep pet pigeons as a child.

SPOT THE DIFFERENCE

Can you find eight differences between the top and bottom pictures?
You can check your answers on page 93.

SUMMER SURPRISE

YOUR VERY OWN LITTLE MIX ADVENTURE STORY IS ABOUT TO BEGIN. READ THE TALE BELOW, THEN CAREFULLY CHOOSE YOUR OPTIONS TO DECIDE WHAT HAPPENS. ENJOY THE ACTION!

It's the summer holidays and you're away with your family in a cottage on the coast. One sunny morning, you go for a walk along the nearby high street. Your mum asks you to be back in 30 minutes. The street is packed with lovely cafés and gift shops. A store selling local ice cream catches your eye and you wander over.

At the counter you order a strawberry cornet with extra sparkles. You open your purse and search through it for a £2 coin. You fish it out, but drop it and the coin rolls across the shop floor. As you scramble after it with your head down, you bump into another customer's legs.

Embarrassed and feeling very clumsy, you look up at the person and get ready to say sorry. But, to your huge surprise, the person standing there is Jade from Little Mix. She smiles sweetly at you as you stand up and try not to hit the floor again in total shock.

If you decide:
1. To talk to Jade, go to **A**, below.
2. To turn away and leave the shop, go to **B**, **page 55**.

A: 'Er, um, hello,' you say to Jade, extremely nervously. 'Sorry to bump into you like that.'

Jade smiles and has a little giggle. 'Don't worry, pet,' she replies in her soothing Geordie accent. 'I can be a bit clumsy, too!' You both laugh. 'Let me buy your ice cream for you,' she offers. 'In fact, I'll have a Strawberry Sparkle, too.'

Still in a daze at meeting one of your idols, you and Jade stroll out of the shop, licking your sweet treats. 'What's your name?' she asks. In a slightly less nervous fashion, you tell Jade your name and that you're on holiday with your family and having a lovely time at the seaside cottage.

'Oh no, that reminds me,' you say out loud. 'My mum said to be back at the cottage in 30 minutes.'

If you decide:
1. To leave and dash back to the cottage, go to **A1**, below.
2. To ask to borrow Jade's phone to message your mum, go to **A2**, **page 53**.

A1: You run back to where you're staying. You are 20 minutes late and think you're going to be told off. 'Where have you been?' your mum says, angrily.

'I bumped into Jade from Little Mix. We both had a Strawberry Sparkle and got talking and I lost track of ...'

Mum interrupts you. 'Jade from Little Mix?' she says, disbelievingly. 'If you're going to be late, please don't make up lies as well. You're grounded for the rest of the day.'

Upset and unable to convince her it's the truth, you go to the bottom of the garden and sulk on the bench. Now you'll never get to go back into town and see if Jade is still there.

If you decide:
1. To hatch a plan to see Jade again, go to **A1a**, below.
2. To just accept your punishment, go to **A1b**, **page 52**.

A1a: You're determined to meet Jade again. After all, she's a Little Mix superstar who you've watched countless times on TV and YouTube. You've admired her for years. You come up with a brilliant plan.

You ask to borrow your older sister's phone. As Jade loves to post social media messages, there's a chance you can search her posts and prove that she is in the same town as you. Scrolling through Jade's channels, you eventually hit the jackpot and find what you're looking for. 'Having a lovely time at the seaside,' Jade says in an Instagram caption that day. She continues with: 'I even had a Strawberry Sparkle with a fan.'

Excited, you show the message to your mum. 'This proves that I did meet Jade,' you explain.

Mum feels very sorry and apologizes for not believing you. Happy that you're no longer grounded, you feel upset that a few hours have passed and you've lost your chance of ever seeing Jade again. You give your sister her phone back.

That evening there's a knock at the cottage door. Mum asks you to answer it, and standing there is Jade. 'Hello, pet,' Jade says with a grin. 'Your mum contacted me on social media to explain what happened. I wanted to call round and cheer you up!'

You look at Mum, look back at Jade, and shout: 'This is the best summer ever!'

The End

A1b: Upset that you've missed the chance to find Jade again in town, you sulk around the cottage. You know that you should have come home on time, but you were so star-struck by Jade that you didn't think about it. Flicking through some Little Mix books and magazines you packed for the holiday, you think of what could have been.

After finishing your dinner at the cottage that night, there's a surprise knock at the door. You trudge over and open it, without even looking up at who's there. The rest of your family all gasp as you open the door. 'Hello,' Jade says. 'I felt so bad when you had to leave in hurry. It was my fault you lost track of time.' Jade explains: 'I knew you were staying in a seaside cottage. There are only six cottages here so I've knocked on all the doors and finally found you.'

Jade comes into your cottage and poses for selfies with you and your family. This is the ultimate holiday surprise for a Little Mix fan.

The End

A2: Jade is so friendly that of course she lets you use her phone so you can message your mum. She doesn't want her worrying because you're late back to the cottage.

The message you send reads: HI MUM, WILL BE BACK IN 10 MINS. JUST HANGING OUT WITH JADE FROM LITTLE MIX!!! OMG! You hand the phone back to Jade and she puts it in her pocket. You carry on chatting together, talking about your favourite Little Mix tunes and dances. The phone then beeps in Jade's pocket, with a message from Mum: WHAT?!? PLEASE DON'T TELL LIES. COME BACK RIGHT AWAY.

Mum clearly doesn't believe that you're having a once-in-a-lifetime chat with Jade and that's the reason you're late.

If you decide:
1. To finally give up and return home, go to **A2a**, **page 54**.
2. To be brave and ask Jade for help, go to **A2b**, **page 54**.

A2a: You reluctantly say goodbye to Jade and trudge back to the cottage. The thought racing through your mind is that you've met your pop star hero, but had it ruined and cut short by your mum. At the cottage, Mum says how disappointed she is that you made up a lie like that.

You don't have the energy to try explaining that it's the truth. Instead, you slope to the bedroom, lie on the bed and a few tears roll down your face. You can't even face playing some Little Mix music as it would bring back memories of having to leave Jade.

A short while later, you hear footsteps racing up the stairs towards your bedroom. Mum bursts into the room, clutching her phone. 'Look, it's a message to me from Jade,' she says excitedly while showing you the screen. 'Jade has sent a picture of herself in the town, proving that you met up. I'm so sorry that I doubted you.'

You reply to Jade together, and ask to meet up again in the high street. Luckily, Jade says yes! Later that day, outside the ice cream shop, the three of you pose for pictures and chat for ages. Jade is so much fun and this is a summer at the seaside that you'll never forget.

The End

A2b: Feeling as if Jade is now one of your best friends and would help you get out of trouble, you grab her hand and begin running back to the cottage. Jade wonders what's happening, but begins to laugh and senses that you have a trick up your sleeve. 'This is fun!' shouts Jade as you both skip along the street.

Back at the cottage, you stand outside the front door. 'Right Jade, you stay just out of sight and wait for my signal,' you instruct. Jade plays along and hides with her back against the wall, just next to the door. You tap on the door – Mum opens it and doesn't look happy.

'Finally, you're back,' she says firmly. 'And these tales about Jade? Honestly, your imagination is too much sometimes.' You stand there in silence, looking at your mum. A few seconds later, you gesture to Jade to jump out and surprise your mum at the door.

'Ta da!' you scream together, waving your hands and pulling a silly face. You both start signing 'Shout Out To My Mum!' as a joke.

Luckily, your mum sees the funny side and can't believe it really is Jade. The three of you have a smoothie together in the garden and pose for selfies. What a summer surprise it has been.

The End

B: Bumping into Jade while scrambling around on the floor for your coin was too cringy for you. You felt you just had to leave the shop as soon as you could. You didn't even get your ice cream!

Outside the shop you're still red with embarrassment and start to walk away. But then you hear a familiar voice – one you've heard on the TV, radio and YouTube loads of times.

'Wait up, pet' says Jade from behind you. Turning around in disbelief, you see Jade standing there, holding the £2 coin that you still hadn't collected from the floor. 'This is your money, isn't it?'

You pluck up the courage to walk over to Jade. You're able to splutter a few words. 'Er, th-hank you,' you mumble, as you collect the coin. 'It is you, isn't it?'

Jade laughs and actually looks a little embarrassed herself. 'Aye pet, it's me, Jade,' she explains in her cute Geordie accent. 'Although sometimes people get me and Jesy mixed up. You must be a Mixer then, yeah?'

If you decide:
1. To say you're a big fan, go to **B1**, below.
2. To play it cool and play down that you're a fan, go to **B2**, **page 58**.

B1: You can't hide your sheer joy at talking to Jade. 'I know all your songs,' you say while clapping your hands together and grinning like a clown. 'I have a Little Mix T-shirt, pyjamas and even Little Mix perfume. I think you're the best group on the planet.'

Jade nods back at you and she begins to stroke her chin, to exaggerate that she's thinking hard. 'Hmmm, do you fancy having some fun?' she asks you with a twinkle in her eye.

'What sort of fun?' you ask, with a cheeky grin to match.

Jade says: 'Meet me back here outside the ice cream shop at 11am tomorrow morning. Is that a deal?'

If you decide:
1. To meet Jade tomorrow, go to **B1a**, below.
2. To chicken out and not meet up again, go to **B1b**, page 58.

B1a: It's a deal. You wave goodbye to Jade and agree to meet again, at 11am in the morning. You walk away in total amazement at the encounter you've just had.

Back at the cottage, you don't tell your parents or your older sister about what's just happened. They wouldn't believe you anyway, would they? The hours seem to drag until bedtime. Finally, the morning comes and you head off to the high street for the meet up with your new friend, Jade.

She's standing there with a rucksack. 'Come with me,' Jade says, as she takes your hand and leads you to a nearby bandstand which looks out over the beach. It's the type of place where big brass bands get together in the summer and entertain people by the sea. Today it's empty and there's no-one around.

'You said you're a big fan?' Jade asks. You nod, then Jade pulls a portable karaoke machine from her bag and switches it on. She also has two microphones. 'Let's sing Little Mix songs together then!' Jade says.

So, the two of you belt out 'Black Magic', 'Power' and lots of other tunes to the passing seagulls and fishing boats. It's a great giggle and an absolutely mind-blowing experience. No other summer will ever have a surprise like this.

The End

B1b: You get very shy again and politely say that you won't be able to meet up again tomorrow. Jade understands, but she can tell that your mind is torn. The two of you say your goodbyes and go your separate ways.

That evening, you still can't believe what had happened earlier on. Talking to Jade from Little Mix? Was it a dream? The next morning, you borrow your older sister's phone and have a quick look at Jade's social media posts. That morning Jade sent a cryptic public message, saying: 'ANYONE FANCY AN ICE CREAM TODAY? MY £2 TREAT' Surely this was directed at you?

You look at your watch. It's 10.55am. You make a snap decision to race from the cottage to the ice cream shop. Sure enough, stood waiting outside is Jade. You rush over and give her a cuddle. 'You made it,' Jade says with a laugh. 'Let's grab an ice cream … and I'll try not to drop the money.' This is your best summer holiday ever.

The End

B2: You decide to act cool and calm around Jade and pretend to not be the huge Little Mix fan that you really are. Well, at least you'll try to be cool and calm – deep down you're actually a bag of nerves!

'You and Jesy? Yeah, I get you two mixed up sometimes too,' you say, which is a lie. 'You're the one from the north-east though, aren't you?'

Jade slowly nods back at you. 'Yep. I guess my accent gives that away.'

After an uncomfortable silence, Jade says: 'Well, if you're not really a Little Mix fan, you won't be interested in a Little Mix party that I'm having this afternoon. Jesy, Perrie and Leigh-Anne will be there too.' Jade turns away, but you're sure you saw a grin on her face.

A party with Little Mix? That would be a dream come true.

If you decide:
1. To admit you are a fan, go to **B2a**, below.
2. To carry on pretending you're not bothered, go to **B2b**, **page 60**.

B2a: 'Wait, Jade', you say to her, as she turns away from you. 'I don't know why I said all of that. I'm really a huge Little Mix fan – I don't know why I pretended not to be. I would love to meet the rest of the group.'

'Gotcha!' Jade says back at you while pointing and jumping. 'I knew that you were fibbing and could tell you were a Mixer from the moment I saw you. Well, from the moment I saw you crawling on your knees!'

You both laugh and see the funny side. After all, you know that Little Mix love playing pranks and having a joke with their fans. You ask her if it's all a big joke. 'It's no joke,' Jade says. She scribbles a secret address on a piece of paper and gives it to you. It's where the Little Mix party is.

That afternoon, you and your family arrive at the party. Jade lets you in and introduces you to the other girls. Your family are just as amazed as you. 'Anyone for ice cream?' asks Jade, winking at you. What a brilliant summer!

The End

B2b: 'That's okay, thanks Jade. I'm busy this afternoon and not that bothered about going to the party,' you say. Of course you want to go, but you've dug yourself into a hole and there's no escape. You'll miss the party of a lifetime.

You have an idea. 'My sister would love to go though. If you tell me where it is I could take her to the party.' Sensing that you're plotting something, Jade gives you the address.

'I'll see your sister later on then, pet,' smiles Jade.

Back at the cottage, your sister is amazed that you have access to the party. When you arrive, Jade opens the door and lets your sister in, before closing it in front of you. Your head drops. Looking through the glass on the door, Jade quickly opens it again. 'Gotcha!' she shouts. It is all just a joke. Jade knows you are a Mixer and welcomes you in to the best summer party ever.

The End

I ♡ LITTLE MIX BECAUSE ...

THERE'S LOTS TO LOVE ABOUT LITTLE MIX,
BUT WHAT DO YOU LOVE ABOUT THEM THE MOST?
READ THE LIST BELOW AND NUMBER THEM FROM
1 TO 8, WITH 1 BEING YOUR FAVOURITE.

♡ They perform at charity gigs and worthwhile causes.

♡ Little Mix empower girls to be strong, confident and happy within themselves.

♡ They write fun songs with catchy lyrics and tunes.

♡ The girls have good business brains and have released clothing and perfume ranges.

♡ They respect their fans and like to pose for selfies with them.

♡ They speak about hard times they've had and encourage people to open up.

♡ They can be a bit cheeky and sometimes pull harmless pranks.

♡ Little Mix are perfectionists, which means they only release songs and albums that they are really happy with.

FACT OR FIB: JADE

ONLY SIX OF THESE NINE STATEMENTS ABOUT JADE ARE TRUE. PUT A TICK IN THE BOX BESIDE EACH STATEMENT THAT YOU THINK IS FACT AND A CROSS IF IT'S A FIB. CHECK YOUR ANSWERS ON **PAGE 93**.

1. Jade's favourite emoticon is the moon face.

2. This pop princess has a fear of clowns.

3. She eats beans on toast every day.

4. Jade has run the London Marathon.

5. Jade first appeared on *The X Factor* in 2008.

6. She can bite her own toenails.

7. Jade has a onesie with her name on it.

8. The Little Mix star has a university degree in maths.

9. One of her heroes is the famous US singer, Diana Ross.

GROUP OR SOLO?

TAKE THIS TEST TO WORK OUT WHETHER YOU'VE GOT
WHAT IT TAKES TO JOIN A GIRL GROUP OR IF YOU'RE
BETTER AS A SOLO ARTIST. TICK A, B OR C AND
FIND OUT YOUR DESTINY ON **PAGE 66**.

1. At school, do you like to be by yourself or hang out
   with friends?

   a. You much prefer to be with your friends because
      someone always has a fun story to share.

   b. Being by yourself is the best because you can decide
      exactly how to spend your breaktimes.

   c. You're not sure. A group of friends is nice, but sometimes
      you like having your own space.

2. When you have to make a decision, do you like others
   to give advice?

   a. Yes. The opinion of others is always helpful.

   b. No. You know your own mind and don't like to be
      swayed otherwise.

   c. It depends. Some decisions are best made as a group.

3. When you dress up for a party, do you like to wear clothes that look similar to your friends' outfits?

    a. Definitely. It's great to blend into a crowd.

    b. Absolutely not. You always want to stand out as an individual.

    c. Not usually, but some clothing advice and tips from other people can be handy.

4. Is appearing before a lot of people scary unless you have friends standing beside you?

    a. It's very scary – safety in numbers is always best!

    b. It doesn't bother you. Being by yourself means you're free to act as you want.

    c. You're confident in public appearances by yourself and with others.

5. When you're away on holiday do you always try to make new friends?

    a. As soon as you arrive on your holiday, you're looking around the campsite or the pool to make new pals.

    b. You're not that bothered. You have your books, magazines and tablet to keep you entertained away from home.

    c. If you meet new friends, that's cool, but you can always message your mates back home.

6. **What type of songs do you sing along to on the radio?**

   a. Anything by groups such as 5 Seconds of Summer, Clean Bandit and (of course!) Little Mix.

   b. Your faves are people like Ariana Grande, Dua Lipa and George Ezra.

   c. A bit of a mix really, from Drake to Years & Years.

7. **Is it more fun to dance by yourself or with lots of people at a disco?**

   a. Dancing with friends is such a laugh.

   b. By yourself, all the time. You can admire your best moves.

   c. With your friends at a school disco but by yourself at home.

8. **What's best, your birthday or Christmas day?**

   a. You like Christmas more, because everyone gets presents that day.

   b. It's all about you on your birthday, which is epic.

   c. Some years your birthday is the best, and others Crimbo comes out on top.

9. **Do you like your make-up to match others or to be different and unique?**

   a. Just like the others, so you can all coordinate.

   b. Being unique shows you have a strong personality.

   c. You might like some make-up tips from your mates, but not all the time.

Turn the page to discover your inner superstar ...

DID YOU TICK ...

MOSTLY As
It seems like you're suited to being in a girl pop group. The friendship, fun and support of the others will bring the best out of your singing and dancing.

MOSTLY Bs
Going solo is the way you're heading. You're too individual and enjoy doing what you want, when you want. Good for you.

MOSTLY Cs
You haven't made up your mind yet. Maybe you'll start off in a girl group, then have an amazing solo singing career.

SECRET STUFF

EVERY SUPER-FAN SHOULD KNOW SOME SPECIAL SECRETS.
READ ON TO DISCOVER A BUNCH OF FUN FACTS AND
REVELATIONS ALL ABOUT THE LITTLE MIX GIRLS.

♥ When Leigh-Anne was younger, she used to look after two chickens.

♥ Jesy was named after a character on the Australian TV show *Home and Away*.

♥ If Jesy could only listen to one song for the rest of her life, she'd choose 'Run the World' by Beyoncé.

♥ Jade likes to do Sudoku puzzles because she says it's good for her brain.

♥ If they could add another member to Little Mix, they would pick singer and rapper Nicki Minaj.

♥ On a date, Perrie likes to be taken to the beach because it's her favourite place in the world.

IDENTIFY THE ALBUM

BY THE SUMMER OF 2018, LITTLE MIX HAD UNLEASHED FOUR INCREDIBLE ALBUMS. THEY ARE *GLORY DAYS*, *GET WEIRD*, *SALUTE* AND *DNA*. YOUR TASK IS TO IDENTIFY WHICH ALBUM THE FOLLOWING TEN SONGS ARE FROM. CHECK YOUR ANSWERS ON **PAGE 94**.

1. Song: 'Power'
   This is a song all about girl power, being strong and making good decisions.

   Album: ....

2. Song: 'Black Magic'
   Little Mix have fun making people feel happy about themselves.

   Album: ....

3. Song: 'Touch'
   'Touch' is a tune that celebrates being in love and having special memories.

   Album: ....

4. Song: 'Love Me Like You'
   It's a sweet song about romance at a high school prom.

   Album: ....

5. Song: 'Move'
   A catchy dance number where the girls keep the boys
   on their toes!
   Album: ....

6. Song: 'Wings'
   It's a song telling people to be positive about
   themselves.
   Album: ....

7. Song: 'How Ya Doin'?'
   A funny song about boys leaving telephone messages
   for the girls.
   Album: ....

8. Song: 'No More Sad Songs'
   Little Mix sing about feeling better after a relationship
   finishes.
   Album: ....

9. Song: 'Little Me'
   The group encourage youngsters to follow their
   dreams and ambitions.
   Album: ....

10. Song: 'Hair'
    A song about moving on from an ex-boyfriend.
    Album: ....

PICK YOUR POP VIDEO

LITTLE MIX'S VIDEOS ARE PACKED WITH TOP POP TUNES AND DAZZLING DANCES. PICK YOUR ANSWERS TO THESE QUESTIONS AND FOLLOW THE ARROWS TO DISCOVER WHICH VIDEO YOU LIKE THE MOST.

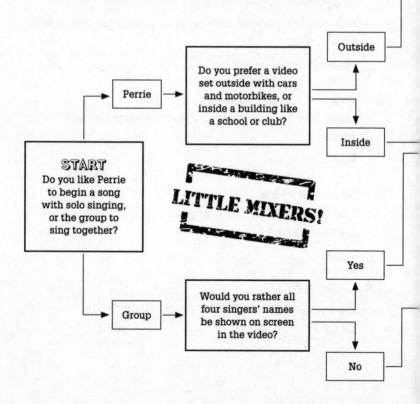

Outside

Perrie → Do you prefer a video set outside with cars and motorbikes, or inside a building like a school or club?

Inside

START
Do you like Perrie to begin a song with solo singing, or the group to sing together?

LITTLE MIXERS!

Yes

Group → Would you rather all four singers' names be shown on screen in the video?

No

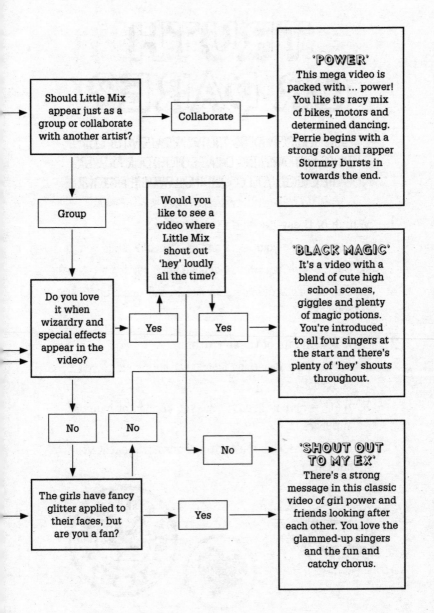

Should Little Mix appear just as a group or collaborate with another artist?

Collaborate

'POWER'
This mega video is packed with ... power! You like its racy mix of bikes, motors and determined dancing. Perrie begins with a strong solo and rapper Stormzy bursts in towards the end.

Group

Would you like to see a video where Little Mix shout out 'hey' loudly all the time?

Do you love it when wizardry and special effects appear in the video?

Yes

Yes

'BLACK MAGIC'
It's a video with a blend of cute high school scenes, giggles and plenty of magic potions. You're introduced to all four singers at the start and there's plenty of 'hey' shouts throughout.

No

No

No

'SHOUT OUT TO MY EX'
There's a strong message in this classic video of girl power and friends looking after each other. You love the glammed-up singers and the fun and catchy chorus.

The girls have fancy glitter applied to their faces, but are you a fan?

Yes

TRUTH OR DARE?

IMAGINE YOU'RE PLAYING TRUTH OR DARE WITH LITTLE MIX. PICK AN ANSWER TO EACH OF THESE AND THINK OF THE LAUGHS YOU COULD HAVE WITH THE GROUP.

1. Which of these dares do you choose?
   a. Dare – close your eyes and let someone tickle you.
   b. Dare – walk backwards around your garden ten times.
   c. Dare – stand outside your house and sing a Little Mix song loudly.

2. Now reveal one of these truths ...
   a. Truth – say something funny that happened to you at school.
   b. Truth – reveal the last time you accidentally burped in public.
   c. Truth – describe the most embarrassing outfit you have worn.

3. Back to the dares! Take your choice from ...

   a. Dare – spend the next hour talking in an Essex accent, like Jesy.

   b. Dare – wear your pyjamas for the rest of the day.

   c. Dare – use an empty loo roll as a microphone and sing a Little Mix tune to a stranger.

4. Truth time again! Pick from ...

   a. Truth – the grossest thing you've ever done.

   b. Truth – the most embarrassing moment with your family.

   c. Truth – the most disgusting thing you've ever eaten.

5. You've got to take a dare. Which will it be?

   a. Dare – fill your mouth with water and sing like Jade.

   b. Dare – tell the stupidest joke you can think of.

   c. Dare – dance to Little Mix, but pretend you're a baby.

6. What truth are you going to make public?

   a. Truth – when you've told a sneaky lie to a friend.

   b. Truth – the most embarrassing object in your bedroom.

   c. Truth – something a teacher has told you off for.

7. The final round of dares. Make your decision from ...

   a. Dare – wear your clothes backwards for a day.

   b. Dare – wear pop star diva sunglasses (at night!).

   c. Dare – tell your friends that Little Mix songs and videos are rubbish.

MIXED UP

CAN YOU FIND ALL 12 LITTLE MIX SONGS HIDDEN
IN THIS GRID? THE SONG TITLES CAN BE IN ALL
DIRECTIONS - UPWARDS, BACKWARDS, FORWARDS,
DOWNWARDS OR DIAGONAL. IF YOU SPOT THEM ALL
IN UNDER THREE MINUTES, YOU'RE AN EAGLE-EYED
FAN. GO TO **PAGE 94** FOR THE ANSWERS.

SHOUT OUT TO MY EX   LOVE ME LIKE YOU

BLACK MAGIC   WINGS

ONLY YOU   DNA

TOUCH   CHANGE YOUR LIFE

SECRET LOVE SONG   POWER

HAIR   OOPS

H	A	U	O	Y	E	K	I	L	E	M	E	V	O	L
O	I	O	U	T	H	S	A	Y	N	M	A	G	I	O
S	E	C	R	E	T	L	O	V	E	S	O	N	G	K
T	G	B	Y	O	U	R	V	C	J	U	L	I	K	E
S	S	H	O	U	T	O	U	T	T	O	M	Y	E	X
O	G	T	O	U	R	F	R	E	G	Y	H	L	Y	L
P	E	N	Y	E	X	T	U	E	W	Y	S	N	A	O
S	T	E	I	R	W	O	Y	O	U	L	O	O	N	V
C	T	H	E	W	G	U	S	E	C	N	N	M	D	E
J	O	N	H	R	V	C	S	P	O	O	G	Y	O	U
E	W	O	I	R	A	H	U	C	R	P	S	E	T	I
V	D	A	S	P	O	L	L	H	L	M	O	I	K	E
E	H	S	P	O	W	K	D	N	E	A	M	W	I	Y
C	H	A	N	G	E	Y	O	U	R	L	I	F	E	J
O	Y	B	B	L	A	C	K	M	A	G	I	C	A	R

HAPPY HALLOWEEN

JUST LIKE LITTLE MIX, YOU LOVE CELEBRATING AND DRESSING UP FOR HALLOWEEN EACH YEAR. FILL IN THE BLANKS TO COMPLETE THIS SPOOKY STORY. CHOOSE FROM THE OPTIONS OR CREATE YOUR OWN SENTENCES.

You and two school friends are getting ready for an evening of trick or treating on 31st October. Halloween is great fun for you all. You've selected your outfits – both of your mates have skeleton suits, but you've chosen to dress as a

.... (zombie/ghost/monster).

It's just getting dark as you step outside your house. The streets are beginning to fill with other groups of people knocking on doors asking for sweets and treats. You're very

.... (excited/nervous/hungry for chocolate). Clutching your torches, you head off among the other Halloween partygoers.

A couple of minutes later, you spy a group of four costumed girls heading towards you. You look at your friends in amazement as you begin to recognize their voices and silhouettes. Could it really be Little Mix hiding under those dark and scary outfits? As the four get nearer, one of them

races to you and shouts '...' (boo/hello/
trick or treat?) What an unbelievable surprise!

'Would you like to join us this evening?' asks one of the
girls. You look a little closer and under the spooky make-up,
you can see that .... (Jade/Jesy/Leigh-Anne/
Perrie) is asking the question.

'Yes please!' you all shout back in unison.

The first house you come to looks a bit creepy. It's an old
.... (castle/cottage/hotel). 'Shall we
knock on the door?' asks .... (Jade/Jesy/
Leigh-Anne/Perrie/one of your friends). You decide to be brave
and knock. A person dressed like an ancient Egyptian in
bandages opens the door.

'...' (Trick or treat/Ahhhhh!/I want
my mummy!) you scream together. Then, the person slowly
takes their mask off.

To your relief, the person reveals themself as ....
(Simon Cowell/your headteacher). You're invited in and before
your eyes is the biggest Halloween party you've ever seen.
'Come on,' you say. 'Let's join in and ask the DJ to play
.... ('Power'/'Black Magic'/'Secret Love Song')
to really get it rocking in here!'

MAKE-UP MISSION

EACH LITTLE MIX GIRL HAS SCRIBBLED A NOTE TO THE BAND'S MAKE-UP ARTIST. IT EXPLAINS THEIR MAKE-UP REQUESTS AND TIPS BEFORE THEIR CONCERT THE NEXT DAY. READ EACH LIST AND WORK OUT WHO WROTE WHICH ONE. THE ANSWERS ARE ON **PAGE 94**.

- Lots of blusher around my cheekbones
- Dark mascara and eyeliner
- Light lipstick to match my red-coloured, dyed hair
- Fierce, dark eyebrows

Written by: ....

- Colours to suit my blonde hair
- Pretty eye shadow around my blue eyes
- Make sure you can see my freckles
- Neutral-colour lipstick

Written by: ....

- Bright red lippie to contrast with my darker skin
- Gentle and calming eye shadow
- Bring out my dark brown eyes
- Defined eyebrows

Written by: ....

- I like a princess look (love Disney princesses!)
- Shades that contrast with my golden hair
- Subtle eye colours
- Make the most of my high cheekbones

Written by: ....

A LITTLE LOOK

THE WORD 'LITTLE' IS HIDDEN IN THIS GRID FIVE TIMES.
IT COULD BE WRITTEN UP, DOWN, FORWARDS, BACKWARDS AND
DIAGONALLY. TURN TO **PAGE 95** TO SEE WHERE THEY ALL ARE.

L	M	A	F	G	T	S	B	A	N	H	O
O	L	M	A	T	R	A	I	S	I	T	L
M	E	I	S	O	U	L	C	P	O	W	I
W	F	K	T	X	I	S	H	A	E	D	T
E	R	H	Q	T	W	P	A	B	L	K	T
G	I	I	T	H	L	D	R	O	T	F	L
C	A	L	F	E	B	E	J	G	T	A	E
D	E	L	I	Y	K	F	L	N	I	M	G
I	G	T	R	C	E	U	P	K	L	B	C
T	X	O	Y	O	D	N	W	M	X	H	O
T	E	P	E	L	T	T	I	L	E	D	U
E	B	A	S	E	O	F	R	A	G	N	E

BLACK MAGIC

GET YOUR PENCIL AT THE READY, BECAUSE YOUR
CHALLENGE IS TO MAKE AS MANY WORDS AS POSSIBLE
FROM THE SONG TITLE 'BLACK MAGIC'. EACH WORD MUST
HAVE AT LEAST THREE LETTERS. SEE **PAGE 95** FOR A LIST.

....

....

....

....

....

....

....

....

....

....

WHO SAID IT?

IF YOU ARE A TRUE SUPER-FAN, YOU HANG ON EVERY WORD THAT PERRIE, JADE, JESY AND LEIGH-ANNE SAY. CAN YOU WORK OUT WHICH ONE OF THE GIRLS SAID THESE QUOTES? CHECK THE ANSWERS ON **PAGE 96.**

1. 'For some reason, every time us Little Mix girls come to America we crave frozen yoghurt!'

Who said it? ....

2. 'As I got older in my teenage years, I thought "maybe I want to be a singer."'

Who said it? ....

3. 'I've got two brothers and one sister. My mum brought us up all on her own – she's amazing.'

Who said it? ....

4. 'I used to do karaoke when I went away on holiday with my family.'

Who said it? ....

5. 'I've never stopped laughing since I've been in this group!'

Who said it? ....

6. 'I had a job in a salon. I used to wash old ladies' hair, mop and sweep and everything. I used to get paid £20 a week.'

Who said it? ....

7. 'I love the girls and I love what we do.'

Who said it? ....

8. 'I love boho, hippie, festival kind of style.'

Who said it? ....

9. 'The word "believe" has always been special to me. Not a lot of people did believe in me at the start.'

Who said it? ....

10. 'I'm a big fan of tattoos. I absolutely love them.'

Who said it? ....

LITTLE MIXERS!

WORD UP

'WORD UP' IS ONE OF LITTLE MIX'S EARLY SONGS. USE THE CLUES BELOW TO HELP YOU COMPLETE THE CROSSWORD, THEN HAVE A LOOK AT **PAGE 96** TO SEE IF YOU'RE CORRECT.

ACROSS

1. Whose nickname used to be Pickle? (4)

2. Where did Jesy grow up? (5)

3. What was the band originally called? (8)

4. Which song is a collaboration with Little Mix and Cheat Codes? (4,3)

5. Whose style inspiration is Gwen Stefani? (4)

DOWN

6. Which of the girls is named after a famous singer? (6)

7. What is the name of the album they released in 2013? (6)

8. What was their debut album? (3)

9. Which show did the girls meet on? (3,1,6)

10. Which of the girls has a phobia of flies? (5-4)

NUMBER CRUNCH

DON'T WORRY – YOU WON'T NEED A CALCULATOR FOR THIS QUIZ! PICKING FROM THE SIX NUMBERS AT THE BOTTOM, CAN YOU ANSWER EACH NUMBER-RELATED QUESTION? THE ANSWERS CAN BE FOUND ON **PAGE 96**.

1. Number of girl bands that had won the UK's *The X Factor* before Little Mix did: ....

2. Number of weeks that 'Cannonball' spent in the UK Top 100 Chart: ....

3. Number in the chart that the single 'Move' peaked at: ....

4. Amount (in British pounds) that Jesy once spent on a handbag: ....

5. Number of views that the official video for 'Your Love' had by August 2018: ....

6. Number of tickets sold for the *Glory Days* tour: ....

3   551,000   900

0   270,495   8

BINGO TIME

FOR THIS GAME YOU'LL NEED SOME PAPER,
SOME PENCILS AND A FRIEND TO PLAY WITH!

HOW TO PLAY:

1. Copy each word or phrase below on to separate scraps of paper. Fold up the paper and put them in a small container.

2. Each player chooses a bingo card on the next pages.

3. Take turns unfolding a piece of paper and reading the word. Both of you need to find the word on your card and cross it off. The first player to cross off a horizontal, vertical or diagonal line of four items and shout 'Little Mix bingo!' wins.

LEIGH-ANNE	MICROPHONE	VIDEO	NUMBER ONE
THE X FACTOR	JESY	SINGING	DANCING
JADE	CHARTS	SPEAKER	PERRIE
CONCERT	DRESSING UP	WORLD TOUR	MUSIC

LITTLE MIX BINGO   PLAYER 1

NAME: ....

LEIGH-ANNE	MICROPHONE	VIDEO	NUMBER ONE
THE X FACTOR	JESY	SINGING	DANCING
JADE	CHARTS	SPEAKER	PERRIE
CONCERT	DRESSING UP	WORLD TOUR	MUSIC

LITTLE MIX BINGO   PLAYER 2

NAME: ....

MICROPHONE	JESY	VIDEO	NUMBER ONE
THE X FACTOR	SPEAKER	PERRIE	MUSIC
DANCING	CONCERT	LEIGH-ANNE	SINGING
CHARTS	DRESSING UP	WORLD TOUR	JADE

COOL COLLABS

LITTLE MIX HAVE JOINED UP WITH MANY OTHER ARTISTS TO MAKE MUSIC. THIS IS KNOWN AS COLLABORATING. FILL IN THE MISSING LETTERS TO COMPLETE THE NAMES OF SOME OF THESE ARTISTS. LOOK FOR THE ANSWERS ON **PAGE 96**.

1. ST_RM_ _

2. CHAR_ _ EP_ _H

3. MIS_YE_ _IO_T

4. C_C_

5. JA_ _ND_RUL_

6. CH_ _TC_D_S

ALL THE ANSWERS

Super-fan-tastic!
Pages 6–8

1. a
2. c
3. a
4. b
5. b
6. c
7. b
8. a
9. a
10. a
11. b
12. c

Fact or Fib: Jesy
Page 9
Numbers two, five and eight are false

The Little Mix Story
Pages 10–11
In order of appearance, the answers are: *The X Factor*,
Little Mix, Rhythmix, 'Cannonball', one, *DNA*, Magic,
Days, Brit Award

Tweet Hearts
Page 12
The mystery Tweeter is Perrie

Song Scramble
Pages 14–15

1. 'Wings'
2. 'Power'
3. 'Touch'
4. 'Shout Out To My Ex'
5. 'Black Magic'
6. 'Hair'
7. 'Salute'
8. 'Love Me Like You'
9. 'Secret Love Song'

Who Said It?
Pages 16–17

1. Perrie
2. Jesy
3. Jade
4. Jesy
5. Leigh-Anne
6. Perrie
7. Jade
8. Leigh-Anne
9. Perrie
10. Jesy

Tweet Hearts
Page 23
The mystery Tweeter is Leigh-Anne

Code Cracker
Pages 24–25
The city is London
The mystery performer is Nicki Minaj
The secret combination is 27 1 2016

Fact or Fib: Leigh-Anne
Page 26
Numbers three, six, eight and nine are false

Super Star Solver
Page 27

Start Singing Now
Pages 30–31

1. Leigh-Anne
2. Perrie
3. All of them
4. Perrie
5. All of them
6. Leigh-Anne
7. All of them
8. Jade
9. Perrie
10. Jesy

Tweet Hearts
Page 34
The mystery Tweeter is Jade

Tweet Hearts
Page 47
The mystery Tweeter is Jesy

Fact or Fib: Perrie
Page 48
Numbers four, eight and nine are false

Spot the Difference
In Picture Section

1. Perrie's lip colour has changed
2. Jesy's necklace is missing a pendant
3. Jesy is missing a ring
4. Leigh-Anne has an extra ring on
5. Leigh-Anne's top is longer
6. Leigh-Anne's nail colour has changed
7. Jade has a pink streak in her hair
8. Jade is missing the gems from her skirt

Fact or Fib: Jade
Page 62
Numbers three, four and eight are false

Identify the Album
Pages 68–69

1. *Glory Days*
2. *Get Weird*
3. *Glory Days*
4. *Get Weird*
5. *Salute*
6. *DNA*
7. *DNA*
8. *Glory Days*
9. *Salute*
10. *Get Weird*

Mixed Up
Pages 74–75

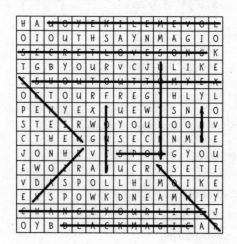

Make-up Mission
Pages 78–79

1. Jesy   2. Perrie   3. Leigh-Anne   4. Jade

A Little Look
Page 80

L	M	A	F	G	T	S	B	A	N	H	O
O	L	M	A	T	R	A	I	S	I	T	I
M	E	I	S	O	U	L	C	P	O	W	I
W	F	K	T	X	I	S	H	A	I	D	I
E	R	H	Q	W	P	A	B	L	K	I	
G	I	I	T	H	L	D	R	O	T	F	I
C	A	L	F	E	B	L	J	G	T	A	I
D	L	L	I	Y	K	F	L	N	M	G	
I	G	T	R	C	E	U	P	K	L	B	C
T	X	O	Y	O	D	N	W	M	X	H	O
T	E	P	L	I	T	T	I	L	E	D	U
E	B	A	S	E	O	F	R	A	G	N	E

Black Magic
Page 81

Some words that can be made from 'Black Magic' include:

CLICK	LACK	LAMB
CLACK	CAB	CALM
LICK	BAG	BIG
MILK	LAG	

Between 0 to 3 words:

Well, you need to start reading the dictionary a lot more!
You can do much better.

Between 4 to 8 words:

Pretty good work, Mixer! You're just as handy with letters
and words as you are with a microphone.

9 and above:

Top marks! You're so good with words you could become
a professional songwriter.

Who Said It?
Pages 82–83

1. Perrie
2. Jade
3. Jesy
4. Leigh-Anne
5. Jesy
6. Perrie
7. Jade
8. Perrie
9. Leigh-Anne
10. Jesy

Word Up
Pages 84–85

Number Crunch
Page 86

1. 0
2. 8
3. 3
4. 900
5. 551,000
6. 270,495

Cool Collabs
Page 90

1. Stormzy
2. Charlie Puth
3. Missy Elliott
4. CNCO
5. Jason Derulo
6. Cheat Codes